KJV

31 DAYS of CELEBRATION

Making Much of JESUS CHRIST
this Christmas Season

A Family Advent Devotional and Ornament Creator
by Sarah Roberts

INTRODUCTION

For unto us a child is born, unto us a son is given: and the government shall be upon his shoulder: and his name shall be called Wonderful, Counsellor, The mighty God, The everlasting Father, The Prince of Peace. Of the increase of his government and peace there shall be no end, upon the throne of David, and upon his kingdom, to order it, and to establish it with judgment and with justice from henceforth even for ever. The zeal of the LORD of hosts will perform this. (Isaiah 9:6-7)

Thank you for joining me in a focused celebration of Jesus Christ during the entire month of December. As you can tell from the Scripture above, there is much about Jesus Christ to celebrate! He is not just worthy of our consideration a couple of times each year, but he is worthy of all our praise and adoration every moment of every day. The purpose of this devotional is to foster a spirit of joyful praise and thanksgiving to God for his greatest gift of all — the gift of himself in the person of Jesus Christ.

I encourage you to make this resource a part of your family's morning routine throughout December. You will begin each day with a unique title or character trait of Jesus Christ along with a key Scripture passage and further study references. Take time to read through the passages together as a family and discuss what you have read. If you have younger children, you may simply choose to read the key passage aloud and talk through some of the very basic truths about Jesus for that day. If you have older children, take turns reading through the entire passages given.

Be sure that you have read through the passages for yourself ahead of time so that you can be ready with specific and directed questions. The goal is to think through how these wonderful truths should affect your day-to-day life. What you believe about God (specifically Jesus Christ) will shape every part of your thoughts, words, and actions. Spaces are provided on each page to write down memorable truths as well as a plan of action to help your family to continue the celebration all day long.

Sharing truths as a family is very important, but responding to God directly about those truths is even more important. Be sure that you take the opportunity to pray aloud your praise, thanksgiving, and confession to God. You may also want to sing a song of praise to God that corresponds with the title of Christ you are studying.

You will find ornament designs in the back of this booklet that can be cut out and used to decorate your tree or another part of your home. Cut them out and place inside fillable clear ball ornaments, or your family can use them to craft your own unique Christmas decorations. There are 36 ornament designs included, and you can choose how and when to use them as part of your advent celebration.

Are you looking for more devotional resources? More devotionals and Bible studies can be purchased from Amazon.com/Author/RobertsSarah. Printable devotional and Scripture memory resources are also available from Etsy.com/Shop/BreathingGrace. I look forward to hearing how your family celebrates Jesus this Christmas season!

In Christ,

Sarah Roberts

CREATOR of the WORLD

Dear JESUS, thank you for creating the universe and everything in it.

For by him were all things created, that are in heaven, and that are in earth, visible and invisible, whether they be thrones, or dominions, or principalities, or powers: all things were created by him, and for him: 17and he is before all things, and by him all things consist. (Colossians 1:16-17)

BREATHE IN GOD'S TRUTH

Colossians 1:15-17; Nehemiah 9:6

Together as a family, read through the Bible passages listed above. Take turns sharing some of the truths about Jesus Christ that you can celebrate today based on what you just read. Write your favorite truth(s) down on the lines below.

....
....
....
....
....
....
....

BREATHE OUT YOUR RESPONSE

Take turns praising God for the truth he has shown you about himself. Write down some practical ways that you can celebrate Jesus Christ as your Creator throughout your day.

....
....
....
....
....
....
....

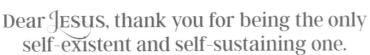

Dear Jesus, thank you for being the only self-existent and self-sustaining one.

Then said the Jews unto him, Thou art not yet fifty years old, and hast thou seen Abraham? Jesus said unto them, Verily, verily, I say unto you, Before Abraham was, I am. (John 8:57-58)

BREATHE IN GOD'S TRUTH
Exodus 3:13-15; John 8:52-59; John 18:4-6

Together as a family, read through the Bible passages listed above. Take turns sharing some of the truths about Jesus Christ that you can celebrate today based on what you just read. Write your favorite truth(s) down on the lines below.

....
....
....
....
....
....
....

BREATHE OUT YOUR RESPONSE

Take turns praising God for the truth he has shown you about himself. Write down some practical ways that you can celebrate Jesus Christ as the Great I Am throughout your day.

....
....
....
....
....
....
....

LORD of HOSTS

Dear Jesus, thank you for being the victorious leader of heavenly armies.

Lift up your heads, O ye gates; And be ye lift up, ye everlasting doors; And the King of glory shall come in. Who is this King of glory? The LORD strong and mighty, the LORD mighty in battle. Lift up your heads, O ye gates; even lift them up, ye everlasting doors; And the King of glory shall come in. Who is this King of glory? The LORD of hosts, he is the King of glory. (Psalm 24:7-10)

BREATHE IN GOD'S TRUTH
Psalm 24; Joshua 5:13-15; Luke 2:13-14

Together as a family, read through the Bible passages listed above. Take turns sharing some of the truths about Jesus Christ that you can celebrate today based on what you just read. Write your favorite truth(s) down on the lines below.

....
....
....
....
....
....
....

BREATHE OUT YOUR RESPONSE

Take turns praising God for the truth he has shown you about himself. Write down some practical ways that you can celebrate Jesus Christ as the Lord of hosts throughout your day.

....
....
....
....
....

Second Adam

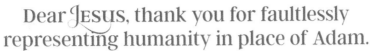

DEC 04

Dear Jesus, thank you for faultlessly representing humanity in place of Adam.

But now is Christ risen from the dead, and become the firstfruits of them that slept.
For since by man came death, by man came also the resurrection of the dead.
For as in Adam all die, even so in Christ shall all be made alive. (1 Corinthians 15:20-22)

BREATHE IN GOD'S TRUTH
Romans 5:12-15; 1 Corinthians 15:42-49

Together as a family, read through the Bible passages listed above. Take turns sharing some of the truths about Jesus Christ that you can celebrate today based on what you just read. Write your favorite truth(s) down on the lines below.

....
....
....
....
....
....
....

BREATHE OUT YOUR RESPONSE

Take turns praising God for the truth he has shown you about himself. Write down some practical ways that you can celebrate Jesus Christ as your Second Adam throughout the day.

....
....
....
....
....
....
....

Root of David

Dear Jesus, thank you for being the fulfillment of each of your promises to David.

And, behold, thou shalt conceive in thy womb, and bring forth a son, and shalt call his name JESUS. He shall be great, and shall be called the Son of the Highest: and the Lord God shall give unto him the throne of his father David: and he shall reign over the house of Jacob for ever; and of his kingdom there shall be no end. (Luke 1:31-33)

BREATHE IN GOD'S TRUTH
2 Samuel 7:8-17; Matthew 1:1; Revelation 5:5

Together as a family, read through the Bible passages listed above. Take turns sharing some of the truths about Jesus Christ that you can celebrate today based on what you just read. Write your favorite truth(s) down on the lines below.

....

....

....

....

....

....

....

BREATHE OUT YOUR RESPONSE

Take turns praising God for the truth he has shown you about himself. Write down some practical ways that you can celebrate Jesus Christ as the root of David throughout your day.

....

....

....

....

....

Dear Jesus, thank you for being entirely God and untouched by sin.

*Then said Mary unto the angel, How shall this be, seeing I know not a man?
And the angel answered and said unto her, The Holy Ghost shall come upon thee,
and the power of the Highest shall overshadow thee: therefore also that holy thing
which shall be born of thee shall be called the Son of God (Luke 1:34-35)*

BREATHE IN GOD'S TRUTH
Romans 1:1-6; 1 John 4:13-16

Together as a family, read through the Bible passages listed above. Take turns sharing some of the truths about Jesus Christ that you can celebrate today based on what you just read. Write your favorite truth(s) down on the lines below.

....

....

....

....

....

....

BREATHE OUT YOUR RESPONSE

Take turns praising God for the truth he has shown you about himself. Write down some practical ways that you can celebrate Jesus Christ as the Son of God throughout your day.

....

....

....

....

....

WORD of GOD

Dear JESUS, thank you for being God's living, complete message of Himself to us.

In the beginning was the Word, and the Word was with God, and the Word was God. The same was in the beginning with God... And the Word was made flesh, and dwelt among us, (and we beheld his glory, the glory as of the only begotten of the Father,) full of grace and truth. (John 1:1-2, 14)

BREATHE IN GOD'S TRUTH

John 1:1-14; 1 Peter 1:23; Romans 10:14-17

Together as a family, read through the Bible passages listed above. Take turns sharing some of the truths about Jesus Christ that you can celebrate today based on what you just read. Write your favorite truth(s) down on the lines below.

....

....

....

....

....

....

BREATHE OUT YOUR RESPONSE

Take turns praising God for the truth he has shown you about himself. Write down some practical ways that you can celebrate Jesus Christ as the living Word of God throughout today.

....

....

....

....

....

DEC 08

Dear Jesus, thank you for displaying the dazzling brilliance of God's glory.

Who being the brightness of his glory, and the express image of his person, and upholding all things by the word of his power, when he had by himself purged our sins, sat down on the right hand of the Majesty on high. (Hebrews 1:3)

BREATHE IN GOD'S TRUTH

Hebrews 1:1-4; 2 Corinthians 4:6; Revelation 1:12-18

Together as a family, read through the Bible passages listed above. Take turns sharing some of the truths about Jesus Christ that you can celebrate today based on what you just read. Write your favorite truth(s) down on the lines below.

....

....

....

....

....

....

....

BREATHE OUT YOUR RESPONSE

Take turns praising God for the truth he has shown you about himself. Write down some practical ways that you can celebrate Jesus Christ as the Radiance of God's glory today.

....

....

....

....

....

....

CHRIST the MESSIAH

Dear Jesus, thank you for being the promised rescuer, infinitely greater than any human prophet or leader.

He saith unto them, But whom say ye that I am? And Simon Peter answered and said, Thou art the Christ, the Son of the living God. And Jesus answered and said unto him, Blessed art thou, Simon Bar-jona: for flesh and blood hath not revealed it unto thee, but my Father which is in heaven. (Matthew 16:15-17)

BREATHE IN GOD'S TRUTH
John 1:40-42; Matthew 23:8-10; 1 John 5:1-5

Together as a family, read through the Bible passages listed above. Take turns sharing some of the truths about Jesus Christ that you can celebrate today based on what you just read. Write your favorite truth(s) down on the lines below.

....
....
....
....
....
....
....

BREATHE OUT YOUR RESPONSE

Take turns praising God for the truth he has shown you about himself. Write down some practical ways that you can celebrate Jesus Christ as the promised Messiah throughout today.

....
....
....
....
....
....

LAMB of GOD

DEC
10

Dear Jesus, thank you for being
the pure and spotless sacrifice for our sins.

And I beheld, and I heard the voice of many angels round about the throne and the beasts and the elders: and the number of them was ten thousand times ten thousand, and thousands of thousands; saying with a loud voice, Worthy is the Lamb that was slain to receive power, and riches, and wisdom, and strength, and honour, and glory, and blessing. (Revelation 5:11-12)

BREATHE IN GOD'S TRUTH
Genesis 22:1-14; John 1:29; Luke 22:7, 14-20

Together as a family, read through the Bible passages listed above. Take turns sharing some of the truths about Jesus Christ that you can celebrate today based on what you just read. Write your favorite truth(s) down on the lines below.

....
....
....
....
....
....

BREATHE OUT YOUR RESPONSE

Take turns praising God for the truth he has shown you about himself. Write down some practical ways that you can celebrate Jesus Christ as the Lamb of God throughout your day.

....
....
....
....
....

GOOD SHEPHERD

Dear JESUS, thank you for gently guiding us as a good shepherd cares for his his sheep.

I am the good shepherd, and know my sheep, and am known of mine.
As the Father knoweth me, even so know I the Father: and I lay down my life for the sheep.
And other sheep I have, which are not of this fold: them also I must bring, and they
shall hear my voice; and there shall be one fold, and one shepherd. (John 10:14-16)

BREATHE IN GOD'S TRUTH
John 10; Psalm 23; 1 Peter 2:24-25

Together as a family, read through the Bible passages listed above. Take turns sharing some of the truths about Jesus Christ that you can celebrate today based on what you just read. Write your favorite truth(s) down on the lines below.

....

....

....

....

....

....

....

BREATHE OUT YOUR RESPONSE

Take turns praising God for the truth he has shown you about himself. Write down some practical ways that you can celebrate Jesus Christ as your shepherd throughout your day.

....

....

....

....

....

DEC 12

Dear Jesus, thank you for being the true light
that exposes and drives out the darkness of sin and death.

Then spake Jesus again unto them, saying, I am the light of the world:
he that followeth me shall not walk in darkness, but shall have the light of life (John 8:12)

BREATHE IN GOD'S TRUTH
John 3:16-21; 1 John 2:7-11

Together as a family, read through the Bible passages listed above. Take turns sharing some of the truths about Jesus Christ that you can celebrate today based on what you just read. Write your favorite truth(s) down on the lines below.

....

....

....

....

....

....

BREATHE OUT YOUR RESPONSE

Take turns praising God for the truth he has shown you about himself. Write down some practical ways that you can celebrate Jesus Christ as the light of the world throughout today.

....

....

....

....

....

....

DEC 13

Bread of Life

Dear Jesus, thank you for sustaining and satisfying us as no one else ever could.

As the living Father hath sent me, and I live by the Father: so he that eateth me, even he shall live by me. This is that bread which came down from heaven: not as your fathers did eat manna, and are dead: he that eateth of this bread shall live for ever. (John 6:57-58)

BREATHE IN GOD'S TRUTH
John 6:22-41; Deuteronomy 8:3

Together as a family, read through the Bible passages listed above. Take turns sharing some of the truths about Jesus Christ that you can celebrate today based on what you just read. Write your favorite truth(s) down on the lines below.

....

....

....

....

....

....

....

BREATHE OUT YOUR RESPONSE

Take turns praising God for the truth he has shown you about himself. Write down some practical ways that you can celebrate Jesus Christ as the bread of life throughout your day.

....

....

....

....

....

....

Truth and the Way

Dear Jesus, thank you for being the source of truth and the only way to the Father.

Jesus saith unto him, I am the way, the truth, and the life: no man cometh unto the Father, but by me. If ye had known me, ye should have known my Father also: and from henceforth ye know him, and have seen him. (John 14:6-7)

BREATHE IN GOD'S TRUTH
John 1:16-18; John 14:1-7

Together as a family, read through the Bible passages listed above. Take turns sharing some of the truths about Jesus Christ that you can celebrate today based on what you just read. Write your favorite truth(s) down on the lines below.

....

....

....

....

....

....

....

BREATHE OUT YOUR RESPONSE

Take turns praising God for the truth he has shown you about himself. Write down some practical ways that you can celebrate Jesus Christ as the truth and the way to God today.

....

....

....

....

....

....

DEC 15

TRUE VINE

Dear Jesus, thank you for nourishing our spirits and empowering us to bear fruit.

Abide in me, and I in you. As the branch cannot bear fruit of itself, except it abide in the vine; no more can ye, except ye abide in me. I am the vine, ye are the branches: He that abideth in me, and I in him, the same bringeth forth much fruit: for without me ye can do nothing. (John 15:4-5)

BREATHE IN GOD'S TRUTH
Psalm 80:7-14; John 15

Together as a family, read through the Bible passages listed above. Take turns sharing some of the truths about Jesus Christ that you can celebrate today based on what you just read. Write your favorite truth(s) down on the lines below.

....
....
....
....
....
....

BREATHE OUT YOUR RESPONSE

Take turns praising God for the truth he has shown you about himself. Write down some practical ways that you can abide in Christ as the vine throughout your day.

....
....
....
....
....
....

DEC 16

Dear Jesus, thank you for sacrificing yourself in love for your undeserving subjects.

Blessed are those servants, whom the lord when he cometh shall find watching: verily I say unto you, that he shall gird himself, and make them to sit down to meat, and will come forth and serve them. (Luke 12:37)

BREATHE IN GOD'S TRUTH
John 13:1-17; Matthew 20:21-28

Together as a family, read through the Bible passages listed above. Take turns sharing some of the truths about Jesus Christ that you can celebrate today based on what you just read. Write your favorite truth(s) down on the lines below.

....
....
....
....
....
....
....

BREATHE OUT YOUR RESPONSE

Take turns praising God for the truth he has shown you about himself. Write down some practical ways that you can celebrate Jesus Christ as your servant king throughout today.

....
....
....
....
....
....
....

DEC 17

Prince of Peace

Dear Jesus, thank you for guarding our hearts and minds with your perfect peace.

Peace I leave with you, my peace I give unto you: not as the world giveth, give I unto you. Let not your heart be troubled, neither let it be afraid. (John 14:27)

BREATHE IN GOD'S TRUTH

Isaiah 26:3-4; Philippians 4:4-7; Romans 16:20

Together as a family, read through the Bible passages listed above. Take turns sharing some of the truths about Jesus Christ that you can celebrate today based on what you just read. Write your favorite truth(s) down on the lines below.

....

....

....

....

....

....

....

BREATHE OUT YOUR RESPONSE

Take turns praising God for the truth he has shown you about himself. Write down some practical ways that you can celebrate the peace you have with the Father through Jesus Christ. How can you allow Jesus Christ's peace to rule in your hearts today?

....

....

....

....

....

....

....

SAVIOUR of the WORLD

DEC 18

Dear Jesus, thank you for rescuing us from sin's power and penalty.

Not by works of righteousness which we have done, but according to his mercy he saved us, by the washing of regeneration, and renewing of the Holy Ghost; which he shed on us abundantly through Jesus Christ our Saviour. (Titus 3:5-6)

BREATHE IN GOD'S TRUTH
Luke 1:46-55; Luke 2:8-14; John 3:17-18

Together as a family, read through the Bible passages listed above. Take turns sharing some of the truths about Jesus Christ that you can celebrate today based on what you just read. Write your favorite truth(s) down on the lines below.

....

....

....

....

....

....

BREATHE OUT YOUR RESPONSE

Take turns praising God for the truth he has shown you about himself. Write down some practical ways that you can celebrate Jesus Christ as your Savior throughout your day.

....

....

....

....

....

....

The RESURRECTION and the LIFE

Dear Jesus, thank you for raising us from death into your everlasting life.

Jesus said unto her, I am the resurrection, and the life: he that believeth in me, though he were dead, yet shall he live: and whosoever liveth and believeth in me shall never die. Believest thou this? She saith unto him, Yea, Lord: I believe that thou art the Christ, the Son of God, which should come into the world. (John 11:25-27)

BREATHE IN GOD'S TRUTH

John 6:38-40; 2 Corinthians 4:13-18

Together as a family, read through the Bible passages listed above. Take turns sharing some of the truths about Jesus Christ that you can celebrate today based on what you just read. Write your favorite truth(s) down on the lines below.

....
....
....
....
....
....

BREATHE OUT YOUR RESPONSE

Take turns praising God for the truth he has shown you about himself. Write down some practical ways that you can celebrate Jesus Christ as the resurrection and the life today.

....
....
....
....
....
....

Blessed Hope

Dear Jesus, thank you for the anticipation of eternal glory and endless delight found in you.

Looking for that blessed hope, and the glorious appearing of the great God and our Saviour Jesus Christ; who gave himself for us, that he might redeem us from all iniquity, and purify unto himself a peculiar people, zealous of good works. (Titus 2:13-14)

BREATHE IN GOD'S TRUTH

Psalm 146; 1 Peter 1:3-9, 13; Colossians 1:24-29

Together as a family, read through the Bible passages listed above. Take turns sharing some of the truths about Jesus Christ that you can celebrate today based on what you just read. Write your favorite truth(s) down on the lines below.

....
....
....
....
....
....
....

BREATHE OUT YOUR RESPONSE

Take turns praising God for the truth he has shown you about himself. Write down some practical ways that you can set your hope fully in Christ throughout your day.

....
....
....
....
....
....
....

DEC 21

Faithful High Priest

Dear Jesus, thank you for being our trustworthy and compassionate mediator.

Seeing then that we have a great high priest, that is passed into the heavens, Jesus the Son of God, let us hold fast our profession. For we have not an high priest which cannot be touched with the feeling of our infirmities; but was in all points tempted like as we are, yet without sin. Let us therefore come boldly unto the throne of grace, that we may obtain mercy, and find grace to help in time of need. (Hebrews 4:14-16)

BREATHE IN GOD'S TRUTH
Hebrews 4:14-5:9; Hebrews 7:18-28

Together as a family, read through the Bible passages listed above. Take turns sharing some of the truths about Jesus Christ that you can celebrate today based on what you just read. Write your favorite truth(s) down on the lines below.

....
....
....
....
....
....

BREATHE OUT YOUR RESPONSE

Take turns praising God for the truth he has shown you about himself. Write down some practical ways that you can celebrate Jesus Christ as your high priest throughout your day.

....
....
....
....
....

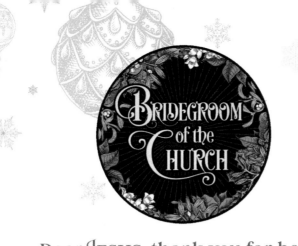

BRIDEGROOM of the CHURCH

DEC 22

Dear Jesus, thank you for being the eternally committed lover of our souls.

Let not your heart be troubled: ye believe in God, believe also in me. In my Father's house are many mansions: if it were not so, I would have told you. I go to prepare a place for you. And if I go and prepare a place for you, I will come again, and receive you unto myself; that where I am, there ye may be also. (John 14:1-3)

BREATHE IN GOD'S TRUTH
John 3:29-30; Ephesians 5:25-33

Together as a family, read through the Bible passages listed above. Take turns sharing some of the truths about Jesus Christ that you can celebrate today based on what you just read. Write your favorite truth(s) down on the lines below.

....

....

....

....

....

....

BREATHE OUT YOUR RESPONSE

Take turns praising God for the truth he has shown you about himself. Write down some practical ways that you can celebrate Jesus Christ as your bridegroom throughout today.

....

....

....

....

WONDERFUL COUNSELOR

Dear Jesus, thank you for being the fountain of all knowledge, wisdom, and discernment.

This also cometh forth from the LORD of hosts, which is wonderful in counsel, and excellent in working. (Isaiah 28:29)

I will bless the LORD, who hath given me counsel: My reins also instruct me in the night seasons. (Psalm 16:7)

BREATHE IN GOD'S TRUTH
Colossians 2:1-3; Romans 11:33-36; Job 12:12-13

Together as a family, read through the Bible passages listed above. Take turns sharing some of the truths about Jesus Christ that you can celebrate today based on what you just read. Write your favorite truth(s) down on the lines below.

....
....
....
....
....
....
....

BREATHE OUT YOUR RESPONSE

Take turns praising God for the truth he has shown you about himself. Write down some practical ways that you can both seek and use the wisdom that Christ gives throughout today.

....
....
....
....
....

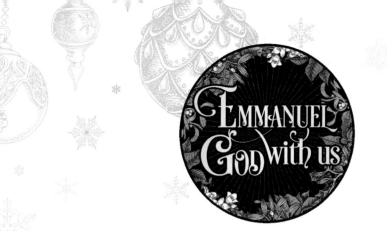

Dear Jesus, thank you for humbling yourself to dwell in love with your creation.

Behold, a virgin shall be with child, and shall bring forth a son,
And they shall call his name Emmanuel. (Matthew 1:23)

BREATHE IN GOD'S TRUTH
Ephesians 2:4-13; Revelation 21:3

Together as a family, read through the Bible passages listed above. Take turns sharing some of the truths about Jesus Christ that you can celebrate today based on what you just read. Write your favorite truth(s) down on the lines below.

....

....

....

....

....

....

BREATHE OUT YOUR RESPONSE

Take turns praising God for the truth he has shown you about himself. Write down some practical ways that you can celebrate Jesus Christ's constant presence throughout your day.

....

....

....

....

....

....

DEC 25

God's Inexpressible Gift

Dear Jesus, thank you for giving yourself, the most unimaginable gift of all.

But now being made free from sin, and become servants to God,
ye have your fruit unto holiness, and the end everlasting life. For the wages of sin is death;
but the gift of God is eternal life through Jesus Christ our Lord. (Romans 6:22-23)

BREATHE IN GOD'S TRUTH

2 Corinthians 9:10-15; Romans 8:31-39

Together as a family, read through the Bible passages listed above. Take turns sharing some of the truths about Jesus Christ that you can celebrate today based on what you just read. Write your favorite truth(s) down on the lines below.

....

....

....

....

....

....

BREATHE OUT YOUR RESPONSE

Take turns praising God for the truth he has shown you about himself. Write down some practical ways that you can celebrate Jesus Christ as the greatest gift of all time.

....

....

....

....

....

....

Dear JESUS, thank you for reigning as the sovereign Lord over all rulers and authorities.

Who is the blessed and only Potentate, the King of kings, and Lord of lords; who only hath immortality, dwelling in the light which no man can approach unto; whom no man hath seen, nor can see: to whom be honour and power everlasting. Amen. (1 Timothy 6:15b-16)

BREATHE IN GOD'S TRUTH
Revelation 1:4-5; Revelation 15:1-4

Together as a family, read through the Bible passages listed above. Take turns sharing some of the truths about Jesus Christ that you can celebrate today based on what you just read. Write your favorite truth(s) down on the lines below.

....

....

....

....

....

....

BREATHE OUT YOUR RESPONSE

Take turns praising God for the truth he has shown you about himself. Write down some practical ways that you can celebrate Jesus Christ as the King of all kings throughout today.

....

....

....

....

....

DEC 27

FOUNDER of our FAITH

Dear Jesus, thank you for granting, strengthening, and protecting our faith.

Looking to Jesus, the founder and perfecter of our faith,
who for the joy that was set before him endured the cross, despising the shame,
and is seated at the right hand of the throne of God. (Hebrews 12:2)

BREATHE IN GOD'S TRUTH
Philippians 1:6; Ephesians 2:8-9; Hebrews 2:10-15

Together as a family, read through the Bible passages listed above. Take turns sharing some of the truths about Jesus Christ that you can celebrate today based on what you just read. Write your favorite truth(s) down on the lines below.

....

....

....

....

....

....

BREATHE OUT YOUR RESPONSE

Take turns praising God for the truth he has shown you about himself. Write down some practical ways that you can celebrate Jesus Christ as the founder of your faith today.

....

....

....

....

....

....

Heir of All Things

Dear Jesus, thank you for being the worthy and rightful owner of all things.

God, who at sundry times and in divers manners spake in time past unto the fathers by the prophets, hath in these last days spoken unto us by his Son, whom he hath appointed heir of all things, by whom also he made the worlds. (Hebrews 1:1-2)

Breathe in God's Truth

Romans 8:12-17; Ephesians 1:3-14; Revelation 5:1-10

Together as a family, read through the Bible passages listed above. Take turns sharing some of the truths about Jesus Christ that you can celebrate today based on what you just read. Write your favorite truth(s) down on the lines below.

....
....
....
....
....
....

Breathe Out Your Response

Take turns praising God for the truth he has shown you about himself. Write down some practical ways that you can celebrate Jesus Christ as the heir of all things today.

....
....
....
....
....
....

FAITHFUL and TRUE

Dear JESUS, thank you that we can rest secure in your untarnished and unchanging nature.

And I saw heaven opened, and behold a white horse; and he that sat upon him was called Faithful and True, and in righteousness he doth judge and make war. His eyes were as a flame of fire, and on his head were many crowns; and he had a name written, that no man knew, but he himself. (Revelation 19:11-12)

BREATHE IN GOD'S TRUTH
Hebrews 3:1-6, 1 John 5:20-21; 2 Timothy 2:1-13

Together as a family, read through the Bible passages listed above. Take turns sharing some of the truths about Jesus Christ that you can celebrate today based on what you just read. Write your favorite truth(s) down on the lines below.

....

....

....

....

....

....

BREATHE OUT YOUR RESPONSE

Take turns praising God for the truth he has shown you about himself. Write down some practical ways that you can celebrate Jesus Christ as always being faithful and true.

....

....

....

....

....

....

Just Judge

Dear Jesus, thank you for the promise that you will one day make all wrongs right.

For as the Father raiseth up the dead, and quickeneth them; even so the Son quickeneth whom he will. For the Father judgeth no man, but hath committed all judgment unto the Son: that all men should honour the Son, even as they honour the Father. He that honoureth not the Son honoureth not the Father which hath sent him. (John 5:21-23)

BREATHE IN GOD'S TRUTH
Romans 2:12-16; Acts 17:24-31; John 5:21-27

Together as a family, read through the Bible passages listed above. Take turns sharing some of the truths about Jesus Christ that you can celebrate today based on what you just read. Write your favorite truth(s) down on the lines below.

....
....
....
....
....
....

BREATHE OUT YOUR RESPONSE

Take turns praising God for the truth he has shown you about himself. Write down some practical ways that you can celebrate Jesus Christ as the rightful, just judge over all the earth.

....
....
....
....
....

DEC 31

EVERLASTING GOD

Dear Jesus, thank you for being eternally worthy of all our adoration.

And when I saw him, I fell at his feet as dead. And he laid his right hand upon me, saying unto me, Fear not; I am the first and the last: I am he that liveth, and was dead; and, behold, I am alive for evermore, Amen; and have the keys of hell and of death. (Revelation 1:17-18)

BREATHE IN GOD'S TRUTH
Isaiah 9:6-7; Hebrews 7:1-3

Together as a family, read through the Bible passages listed above. Take turns sharing some of the truths about Jesus Christ that you can celebrate today based on what you just read. Write your favorite truth(s) down on the lines below.

....
....
....
....
....
....
....

BREATHE OUT YOUR RESPONSE

Take turns praising God for the truth he has shown you about himself. Write down some practical ways that you can celebrate Jesus Christ as the eternal God of the universe.

....
....
....
....
....
....

Creator of the World

The Great I Am

Lord of Hosts

Second Adam

Root of David

Son of God

Word of God

Radiance of God's Glory

Christ the Messiah

Lamb of God

Good Shepherd

Light of the World

Each ornament is approximately 2.5" in diameter.
You can find more digital ornament templates
at Etsy.com/Shop/BreathingGrace.

I would love to see your finished ornament designs!
Please share a picture of your completed ornaments
within a review on Amazon or at Facebook.com/GraceDeclared.

Bread of Life

Truth and the Way

True Vine

Servant King

Prince of Peace

Savior of the World

The Resurrection and the Life

Blessed Hope

Faithful High Priest

Bridegroom of the Church

Wonderful Counselor

Immanuel God with us

Each ornament is approximately 2.5" in diameter.
You can find more digital ornament templates
at <u>Etsy.com/Shop/BreathingGrace</u>.

I would love to see your finished ornament designs!
Please share a picture of your completed ornaments
within a review on Amazon or at <u>Facebook.com/GraceDeclared</u>.

Made in the USA
Middletown, DE
19 October 2023

41074290R00022